Inventions That Help Us at Home

They said it!

'Everything that can be invented has been invented.'

Charles Duell, head of the US patent office, 1899

Aerosol can

An aerosol can is a spray can. When you push the button on the can, the liquid inside comes out as a spray or foam.

Who invented the aerosol can?

A Norwegian, Erik Rotheim, invented the aerosol can in 1926.

The aerosol can story

Erik Rotheim was looking for a way to quickly apply an even coat of wax to his skis. He experimented in his workshop and eventually invented the aerosol can. In 1927 he decided to **patent** the invention. Another Norwegian called Alf Bjerke was the first person to sell aerosol cans in the 1930s.

By the 1940s and 1950s aerosol cans were very popular. They are now used for many products including deodorant, hairspray, paint, cooking oil and even cream.

Pressing the button on top of the aerosol can makes the contents spray out.

Did you know?

In 1998 the Norwegian government honoured Erik Rotheim by issuing a postage stamp with a spray can on it.

How aerosol cans work

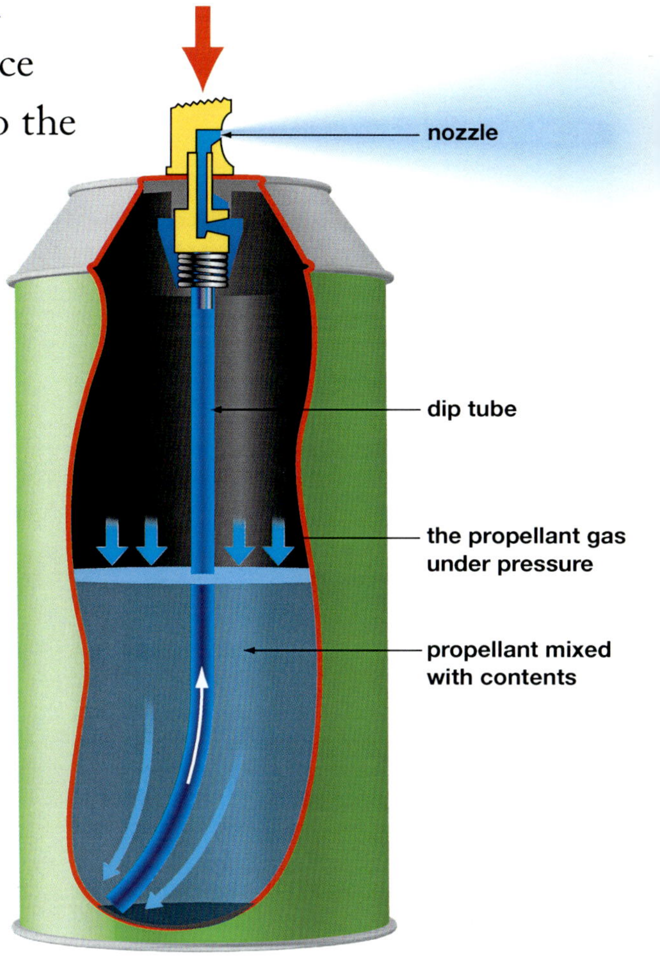

Aerosol cans work due to a substance called a 'propellant'. It is forced into the can under pressure and mixes with the other liquid, such as paint. When you push the button on the top of the can, the propellant rushes out through the dip tube, bringing fine drops of the other liquid with it.

Changes to aerosols over time

Up until the 1970s, a group of substances called chlorofluorocarbons (CFCs) were used as propellants. CFCs were harmful to the environment and they are now banned in most countries. Safer propellants are now used and pump spray packs that contain no propellants are becoming more popular.

Related invention

An Australian burns expert, Dr Fiona Wood, invented an aerosol spray using a patient's own skin. This spray-on skin is used to treat people who have been very badly burned.

BAND-AID®

A BAND-AID® is a type of adhesive bandage strip with a cotton gauze section in the middle.

Who invented the BAND-AID®?

American Earle Dickson invented adhesive bandage strips in 1920. He worked for a company called Johnson & Johnson, who manufactured surgical dressings.

The BAND-AID® story

Earle Dickson's wife Josephine was rather clumsy and often cut her fingers. Earle would put some cotton gauze on the wound and then hold it in place with a sticky cloth bandage.

Earle decided to put some cotton squares at regular intervals along a strip of sticky cloth bandage. Josephine was then able to cut off strips when she needed them. Earle told his boss about his idea and soon the bandages were being made with the brand name BAND-AID®.

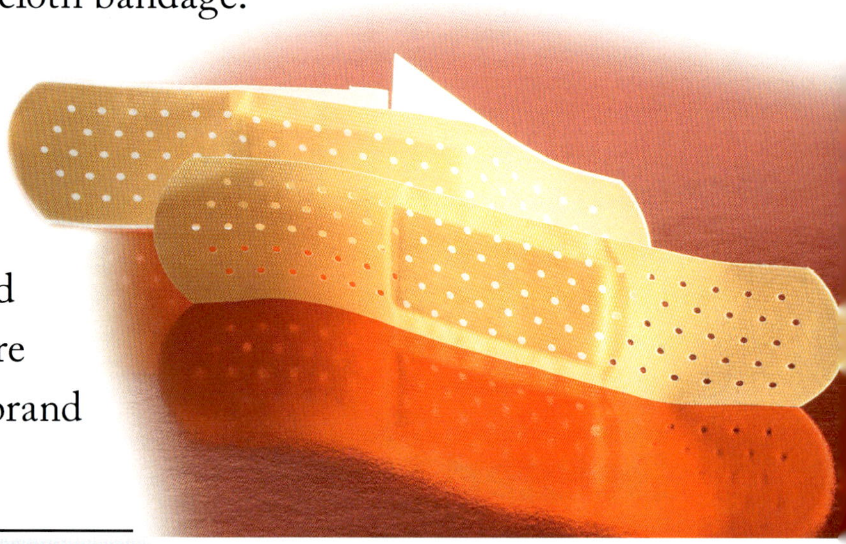

A BAND-AID® has a cotton square in the middle, and air holes all over it.

Did you know?

Cooks in food industries use blue BAND-AID®s. If they fall into food they are easy to see and remove.

How BAND-AID®s work

BAND-AID®s stop dirt, water and germs from entering the wound and causing infections. This helps your body to heal cuts and scrapes. They also cushion the wound to help your body repair the damage caused by the injury.

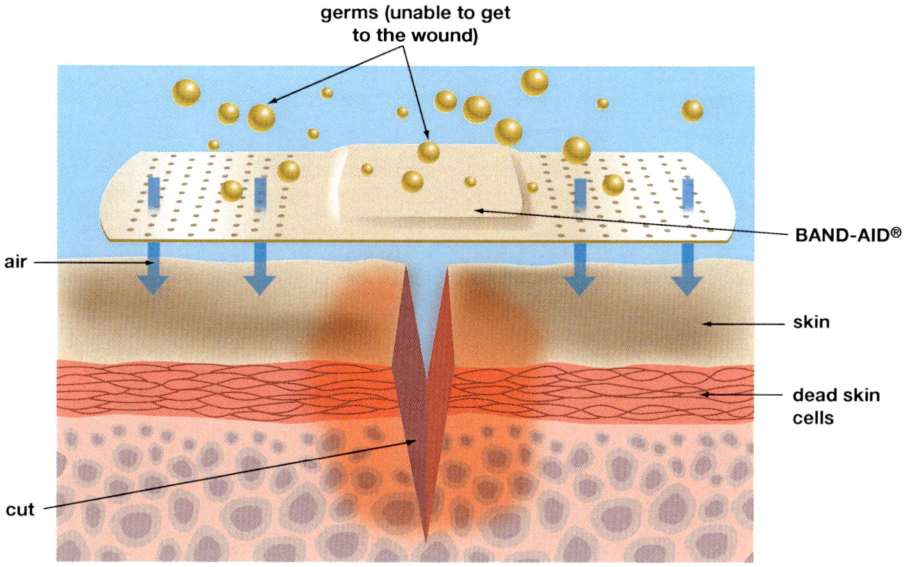

A BAND-AID® protects and helps to heal wounds.

Changes to BAND-AID®s over time

BAND-AID®s now come in a range of sizes and shapes. They are made of plastic and have air holes. These allow oxygen to reach the wound which helps the healing process. Liquid BAND-AID®s can form a seal over the wound without the need for plastic.

Related invention

Spray-on bandages might soon replace adhesive bandages. The spray was invented in 2002. It makes a fine web of fibres that block the wound and give a structure that new skin cells can grow on.

Glossary word

patent a right granted to make, use or sell something which is new, inventive and useful

Battery

A battery is a portable and easy way of providing energy for electrical items. They come in many shapes and sizes, depending on the tasks they are needed for.

Who invented the battery?

Italian scientist, Alessandro Volta, invented the first workable battery in 1800.

The battery story

Twitching frogs' legs gave Volta the idea for the battery. In 1790, his friend Luigi Galvani noticed that a freshly cut frog's leg would twitch when it made contact with two different metals. Volta believed that this effect was due to electricity.

He discovered that when different kinds of metal were put in salty water they produced electricity. The first battery he made was a stack of metal discs separated by pieces of cardboard soaked with salty water.

Batteries come in many sizes, depending on the job they have to do.

Battery timeline

1800	1859	1881	1889	1954
Volta invented the first battery	The lead-acid battery that is used in cars was developed	The type of battery that powers today's torches and radios was invented	Rechargeable batteries were invented	Solar cells were invented

How batteries work

Batteries convert chemical energy into electricity. A regular torch battery has two **electrodes** that are separated by a thick black chemical paste. One electrode is the body of the battery, which is a zinc cup. The other electrode is a carbon rod in the middle of the battery. When you turn on a torch, the reaction between the paste and the zinc cup creates electricity. Electricity flows from one electrode through the light bulb and into the other electrode.

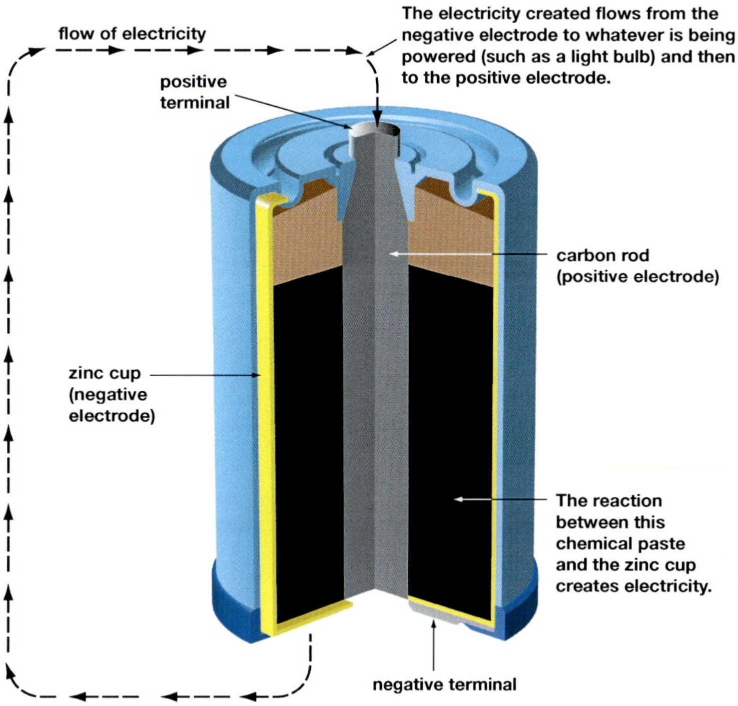

Changes to batteries over time

Batteries that can be recharged have been developed. This reduces the number of batteries being thrown away and harming the environment because of their chemical content. Some batteries use different chemicals and last longer than regular zinc-carbon batteries.

Related invention

Fuel cells are another way of converting chemical energy into electricity. William Grove invented the fuel cell in 1839. Fuel cells use oxygen and hydrogen to make electricity.

Glossary word

electrodes parts of a battery where electricity comes out or goes in

Compact disc

A compact disc (CD) is a moulded plastic disc with a thin film of aluminium on the back. It is used to store music or information.

Who invented the compact disc?

An American, James Russell, invented the compact disc in the 1960s.

The compact disc story

James Russell liked listening to music on vinyl records, but he did not like it when the records were worn out or scratched. He invented a sound playback system where light was used to record and play back the music.

Russell knew that any information could be converted into a series of the digits one and zero. This is how computers handle information. He realised that if he could represent the zeros and ones with dark and light, then he could make a device that could play back sounds. He was able to achieve his goals by using the newly invented laser.

Compact discs can store music and data.

Did you know?

Russell sold his idea to the Dutch electronics company Philips and the Japanese Sony Corporation.

How compact discs work

When music is stored on a compact disc it is converted into an electrical signal and then a series of ones and zeros.

This is then recorded on the surface of the compact disc. Where a one occurs, a pit is burned onto the surface of the disc by a laser. Where a zero occurs no hole is burned, leaving 'land'.

A beam of laser light is then shone onto the disc. It reflects back from the lands but not from the pits. The light is turned into an electrical signal by a computer and then back into music.

Music or information on a CD is stored as a series of pits in a thin film of aluminium.

Changes to compact discs over time

Compact discs can now be made on personal computers either by copying other CDs, downloading files from the Internet or by making your own files.

Related invention

The DVD (Digital Versatile Disc) was invented in 1995. It can store much more information than a CD. It is used for playing movies and storing files from computers.

Frozen food

Frozen foods are foods that are kept at very cold temperatures to prevent them from rotting.

Who invented frozen food?

Clarence Birdseye, an American, invented frozen foods in the 1920s.

The frozen food story

In the early 1900s, Clarence Birdseye, a businessman from the United States travelled to the cold northern Canadian town of Labrador. He noticed that it was so cold that fish and other food froze very quickly. The people kept frozen food to use when fresh food was not available. He had the idea of freezing food in small packets to be used in the home. Although he was not the first person to freeze foods, he invented a way to freeze food that kept in the flavour. His first frozen foods went on the market in 1930.

There are hundreds of different frozen foods available today.

Did you know?

Clarence Birdseye also invented infra-red heat lamps and a way of making paper from sugar cane pulp.

How frozen foods work

Bacteria causes food to rot. If you keep food in the refrigerator, the bacteria slow down and rotting takes much longer. If you freeze food to minus 18°C, the bacteria stop working and you can keep food for a long time.

Freezing does not kill the bacteria, they are only stopped from growing. As soon as you start to thaw out the food the bacteria begin to grow again and the food will start to rot.

Astronauts enjoy freeze-dried ice cream.

Changes to frozen foods over time

Another way to preserve food is to 'freeze dry' it. Food is frozen and then placed in a strong vacuum to suck out all the water. Instant coffee is made by freeze drying. Astronauts and campers also use freeze dried food because it is much lighter to carry.

Related inventions

The frozen 'TV dinner' was invented by Gerry Thomas in 1954. A TV dinner is a whole meal arranged neatly in a divided metal tray. In the first year they were on sale, more than 10 000 000 TV dinners were sold.

Light bulb

A light bulb uses electricity to make light.

Who invented the light bulb?

Two people developed a working electric light bulb at about the same time. They were an English scientist, Joseph Swan, and an American inventor, Thomas Edison.

The light bulb story

In 1878 Joseph Swan made the first globe, but could not stop it from burning out.

One year later, Thomas Edison made a light bulb that worked for 40 hours. The **filament** was made from a piece of burned cotton. It glowed in a bulb that had all the air pumped from it.

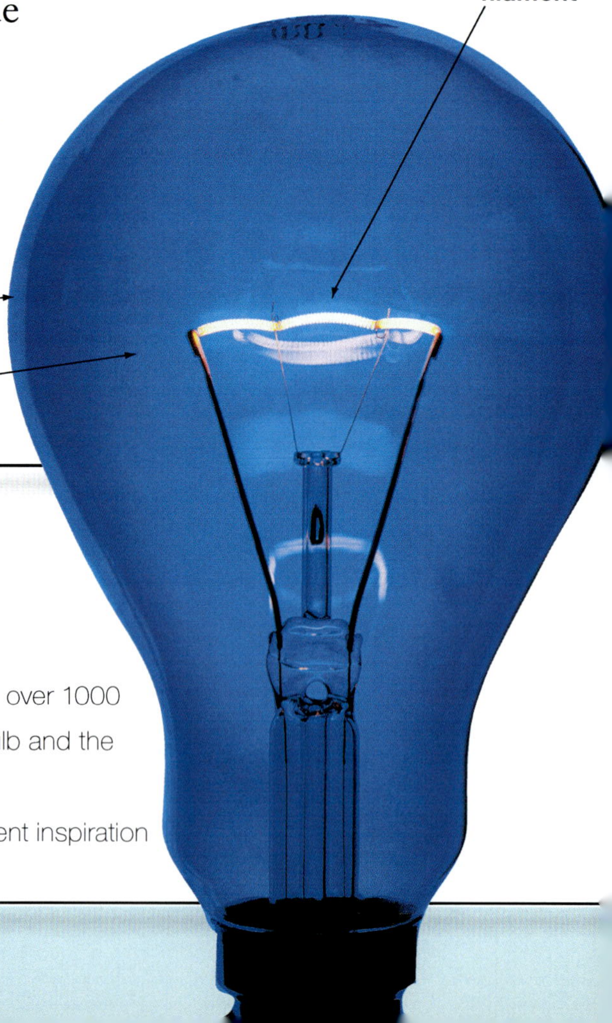

Thomas Edison (1847–1931)

Thomas Edison was expelled from school but became one of the most famous inventors in history. He created over 1000 inventions including the electric light bulb and the phonograph.

Edison said that genius was one per cent inspiration and ninety-nine per cent perspiration.

How a light bulb works

Electricity runs through a thin, coiled piece of wire called a filament. The filament gets very hot (over 2500°C). This makes it give off heat and light. The filament does not catch fire because the globe has an **inert** gas in it that will not let the filament burn.

Changes to light bulbs over time

Light bulbs come in all shapes and sizes, from tiny torch bulbs to giant lighthouse bulbs. Halogen light bulbs contain special gases that let the filament operate at higher temperatures. This makes them more energy efficient.

This light tower at the Melbourne Cricket Ground has 140 light bulbs.

Related invention

Neon lights were invented by Georges Claude in 1910.

Glossary words

filament a thin piece of a certain substance
inert unable to take part in chemical reactions

Liquid paper®

Liquid paper® is a quick-drying paint that is used to cover mistakes on printed or written pages.

Who invented Liquid paper®?

Liquid paper® was invented by an American, Bette Nesmith Graham, in 1951.

The Liquid paper® story

Bette Nesmith Graham wanted to be an artist, but she had to work as a secretary to support her son. She liked her typing to be perfect, with no mistakes. One day she went home and mixed some paint to match the colour of the paper she was typing on. She took a little bottle of the paint and a paintbrush to work and used it to cover up her mistakes. Other secretaries asked for some of her paint and soon she was making and selling it from her home.

Liquid paper® was the first correction fluid to be invented.

Liquid paper® timeline

1951	1956	1968	1990
Bette Nesmith Graham invented correction fluid	Bette Nesmith Graham started the Mistake Out company	The name of the company was changed to Liquid paper® corporation	The first correction pen was sold

How Liquid paper® works

Liquid paper® has to be completely dry before you can write or type over it, otherwise it smudges. The first correction fluid was made by adding powdered white paint to water. The water evaporated slowly so it took a long time to dry out.

The formula was changed and a type of liquid which evaporated much faster than water was used. Correction fluid now dries very quickly.

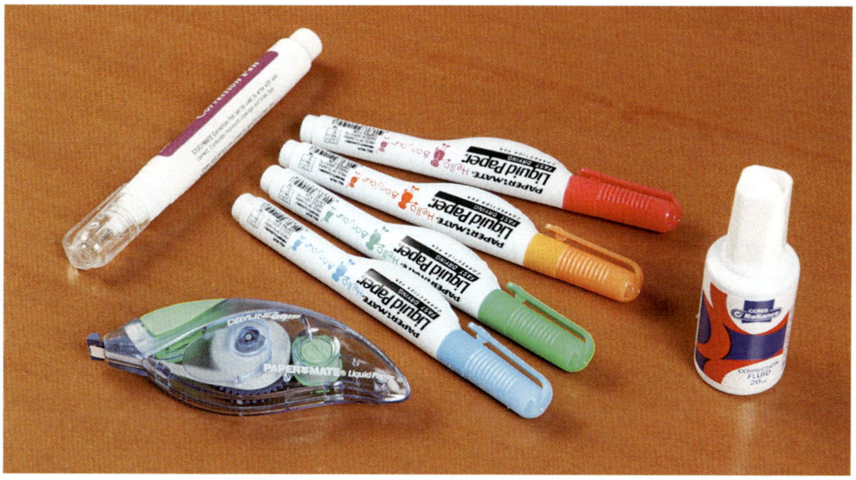

Many types of correction products are now available.

Changes to Liquid paper® over time

Liquid paper® was a very important office tool when most people used typewriters. Now that computers are used instead, correction fluid is not used so often. This is because you can check for mistakes on screen before you print out your work.

Related invention

Bette Nesmith Graham set up two foundations to help women find new ways to earn a living.

Match

A match is a thin piece of wood coated at one end with a chemical. When the coated end, called the head, is rubbed against a rough surface, it catches fire.

Who invented the match?

John Walker, an English pharmacist, invented the match in 1827.

The match story

Before the invention of matches, people would start fires by striking a piece of hard rock called flint with a piece of steel. This would produce a spark which could be used to start a fire.

John Walker's match had a mix of chemicals in its head. It would catch fire when rubbed against paper coated with ground glass.

In 1830 a Frenchman, Charles Sauria, adapted Walker's match by putting white phosphorus in the head. The match worked better, but it was dangerous.

Friction between the match and the side of the box makes it catch fire.

Did you know?

White phosphorus attacks the bones, especially in the jaw. Thousands of people working in match factories were killed or maimed because of white phosphorus poisoning. White phosphorus was replaced in matches in 1911.

How matches work

Matches have part of the burning material on the head and part on the side of the box. This reduces the chance that the matches will accidentally catch fire. The head of a match contains the chemical potassium chlorate. Red phosphorus is glued to the side of the box. When they are rubbed together, the friction creates heat and starts a chemical reaction between the substances. This sets fire to the wood.

Safety matches do not explode in your pocket.

Changes to matches over time

You can now buy matches that are waterproof. These are useful when camping or taking part in water activities, like canoeing.

Related invention

In 1928, Louis Aronson invented a lighter that was fuelled by gas. Once it was lit, it would stay alight until the gas supply to the flame was stopped.

Non-stick pan

Non-stick pans are saucepans and frying pans that are coated with a special plastic called Teflon®.

Who invented the non-stick pan?

The non-stick pan was invented by Marc Gregoire, in 1954 in France.

The non-stick pan story

In 1938 an American scientist, Dr Roy Plunkett, accidentally discovered Teflon®. He was experimenting with different gases and left one batch overnight in a container. When he arrived the next day, the container was filled with a very slippery solid which could not be changed by chemicals. This solid was tetrafluoroethylene, which Dr Plunkett called Teflon®.

In the early 1950s, a Frenchman, Marc Gregoire, learned of Teflon® and put it on his fishing tackle to stop it tangling. His wife came up with the idea of putting it on pots and pans. Gregoire coated one of her frying pans with great success. In a few years, he was selling more than a million non-stick pans a year.

An egg easily slips off a non-stick pan.

Did you know?

The *Guinness World Records* lists Teflon® as the slipperiest substance on Earth.

How non-stick pans work

The coating on non-stick pans is much more slippery than the metal underneath. If you looked at the surface of a metal pan under a strong microscope, you would see small grooves and holes which the food sticks to. A coating of Teflon® fills in all the grooves and holes, making a smooth and slippery surface so there is no way for the food to stick to the pan.

Teflon® coating is sprayed on so that it covers the surface evenly.

Changes to non-stick pans over time

Since the invention of Teflon®, new non-stick coatings have been invented. One is a mixture of titanium metal with **ceramics** that is sandblasted onto the pan. It is then fired to 20 000°C and coated with a non-stick material. These pans last a lifetime, but they are very expensive.

Related invention

Teflon® is used to keep clothing and carpets looking newer for longer. It is also used to make space suits.

Glossary word

ceramics materials such as china that have to be fired in a kiln

Post-it® Note

Post-it® Notes are small notes that have a strip of glue along one edge. The glue can be easily separated and reused many times.

Who invented Post-it® Notes?

Dr Spencer Silver and Art Fry invented Post-it® Notes in the United States between 1968 and 1974.

The Post-it® Notes story

In 1968, Dr Spencer Silver was trying to make very sticky glue for a company called 3M. He accidentally developed a semi-sticky glue instead. This glue could be re-used without leaving sticky bits behind when it was peeled off.

Meanwhile Art Fry, another worker at 3M, was singing in his church choir and worrying about how to stop the bookmarks slipping out of his hymn book. He used Dr Silver's glue to produce sticky bookmarks that could be peeled off and used again. One year later, the 3M company started to make Post-it® Notes.

Post-it® Notes glue was invented by accident.

Did you know?

In 2002, an American artist called Vanalyne Green created a portrait of a cat called Juno using 50 000 Post-it® Notes. It measured 9 metres by 9 metres.

How Post-it® Notes work

For glue to stick properly, it has to completely cover the surface you are sticking. Post-it® Note glue works because it doesn't cover the surface well. This glue is called a **microsphere** adhesive. The tiny balls in the glue are separated with gaps between them. So, although each ball of glue is very sticky, the notes do not stick very strongly overall.

Post-it® Notes now come in many varieties and can be used for many purposes.

Changes to Post-it® Notes over time

An electronic version of Post-it® Notes is available for personal computers. Each note can fit about 32 000 characters. This is about as many characters as there are in this whole book!

Super Sticky Post-it® Notes are now available which can stick on virtually any surface. The Super Sticky Post-it® Notes use a new type of glue which is stronger than the one used on standard Post-it® Notes.

Related invention

In 1902, an Australian stationery company, Birchall's of Launceston, invented the first notepad.

Glossary word

microsphere very small ball

Sticky tape

Sticky tape is a clear tape that has a coating of glue on one side.

Who invented sticky tape?

Sticky tape was invented by Richard Drew, in the United States in 1930.

The sticky tape story

Richard Drew worked for the 3M company, researching sandpaper. One day he went to a car painting factory to test out the sandpaper. He noticed that the painters were painting two different colours on the cars. To get a straight line between the two colours, they protected the first colour using glue and newspaper. But often when they took it off, the paint would come off with the glue. In 1923 he invented some tape for the painters. It was a wide paper tape with glue only on the edges, not in the middle. In 1930 he improved this, by using clear cellophane instead of paper.

Most sticky tape is clear.

Did you know?

One of the early uses for sticky tape was to mend slightly cracked eggs, so that they would not go bad.

How sticky tape works

The glue on sticky tape is a pressure-sensitive **adhesive**. This means that when you press it down hard, it sticks better. If you looked at the sticky side under a microscope, you would see it is not smooth. It has mountains and valleys. When the tape is stuck to an object, bubbles of air are trapped in the valleys. When you try to pull the tape off, the bubbles act like suction cups.

The tape dispenser was invented in 1932.

Changes to sticky tape over time

There are now many different sorts of sticky tape for many different uses. By changing the stickiness of the glue and the type of backing material, sticky tape can be designed for different situations. One sort of sticky tape can be used by doctors to close wounds, instead of using stitches.

Related inventions

The first sticky tape dispenser was invented by John Borden in 1932.

Glossary word

adhesive another word for glue or a sticky substance

Vegemite®

Vegemite® is a spreadable paste that is very popular in Australia.

Who invented Vegemite®?

Vegemite® was invented by an Australian, Dr Cyril Callister, in 1923.

The Vegemite® story

In 1922, Fred Walker wanted to find a way of using **yeast** that was left over from making beer. Yeast is a very good source of vitamin B, and it was very cheap. He employed Dr Cyril Callister to find a use for the yeast. After months of experimenting, Dr Callister came up with a tasty spread. It was first sold in 1923, but it was not popular. Fred Walker gave away jars of Vegemite® with other products and tried changing its name. It wasn't until 15 years after it was invented that it became a popular and successful product.

Australians love Vegemite® sandwiches.

Did you know?

In April 1984, Vegemite® was the first product to be electronically scanned at a supermarket in Australia.

How Vegemite® works

Yeast contains a lot of vitamin B, so it is good for your health, but it does not taste very good. To make Vegemite®, the yeast is mixed in warm water and left to break down so that the vitamin B dissolves into the water. The mixture then thickens and salt and flavours are added.

Vegemite® is sold in tubes for Australian travellers.

Changes to Vegemite® over time

Vegemite® has become very popular in Australia, but not many other counties sell it. Australians travelling to other countries often take a jar of Vegemite®, but it can break in their luggage. To overcome this problem, Vegemite® was packaged in plastic tubes in 1999.

Related invention

A similar spread, Marmite, was invented in England in 1902.

Glossary word

yeast a microscopic kind of fungus that lives naturally on fruit

Velcro®

Velcro® is a hook and loop fastening system. It has many uses, including on clothing, sports shoes and wallets.

Who invented Velcro®?

Velcro® was invented by a Swiss man, Georges de Mestral, in 1951.

The Velcro® story

One day in the summer of 1948, Georges de Mestral was walking with his dog in the countryside. Both he and his dog came home covered in burrs, the prickly seed pods from plants they had brushed against. He examined them under a microscope. He saw that the burrs were covered in tiny hooks that latched around the loops of fabric on his trousers. He decided to invent a fastener that worked the same way.

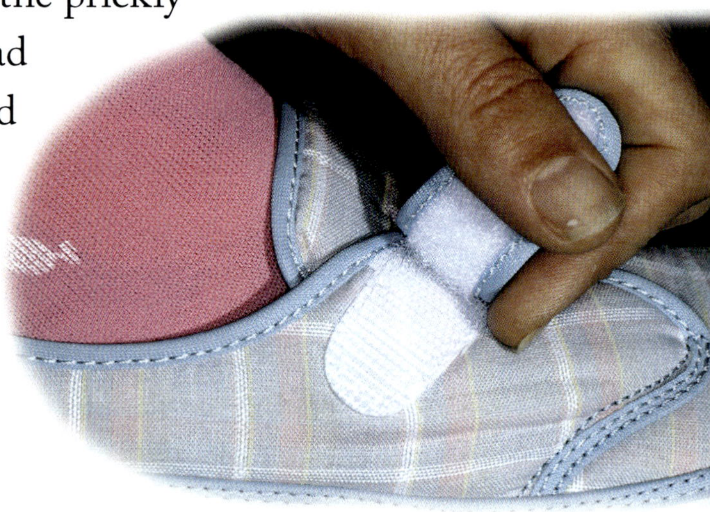

Velcro® can be used on all sorts of clothing.

Georges de Mestral (1907–1990)

Georges de Mestral was born in 1907. As a boy he was interested in nature and inventing. He decided to become an engineer and worked for a Swiss engineering company. After he invented Velcro®, he set up his own company in 1952.

How Velcro® works

One side of the Velcro® is made from tape that has been sewn with nylon. When it is put under a special infra-red light, the nylon forms tough hooks. The other side of the tape is sewn with a soft fuzzy material. When the two sides are pressed together, the hooks latch onto the fuzzy loops.

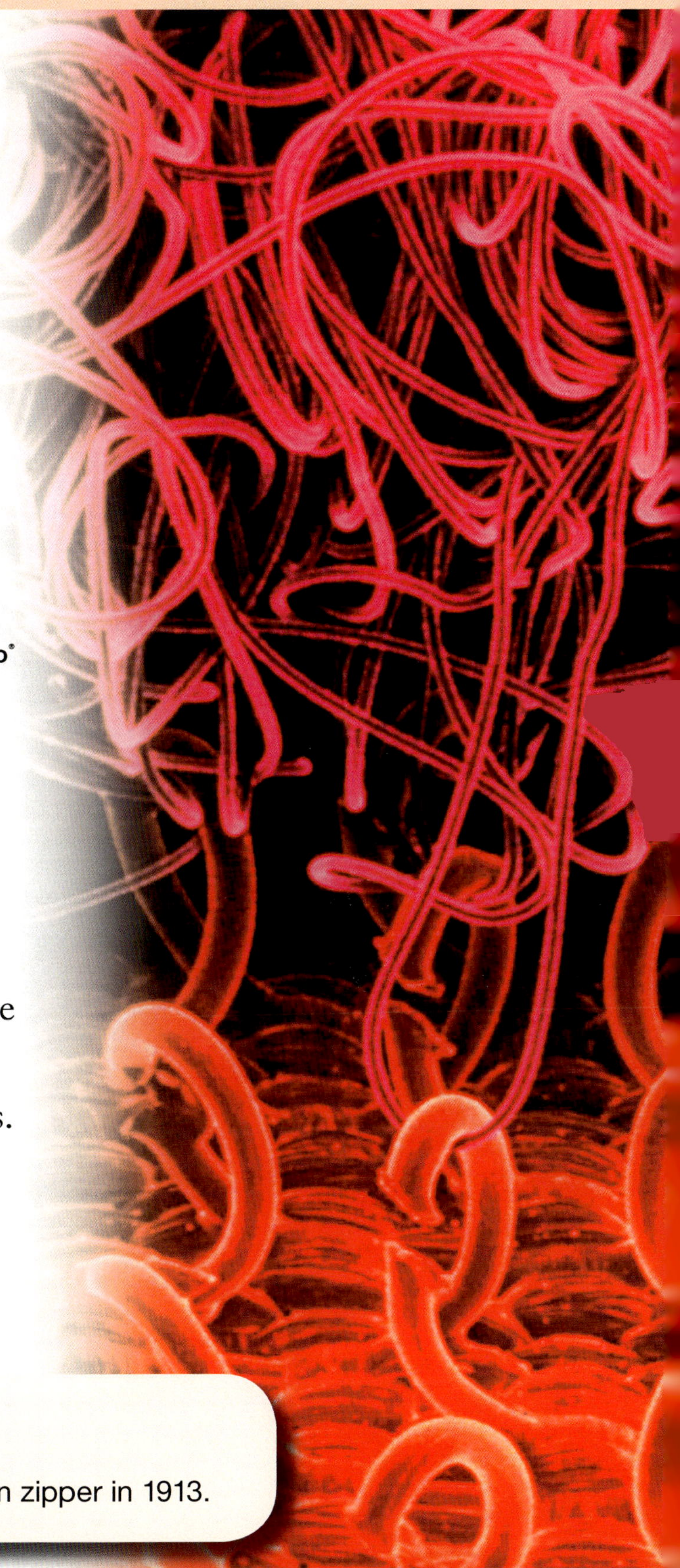

This picture of Velcro® was taken using a microscope.

Changes to Velcro® over time

The first Velcro® tape could only be sewn onto other fabrics. Now it can be stuck onto solid things like notice boards. Space suits have Velcro® fastenings and attachments for tools. The big gloves that astronauts wear make using zippers and buckles impossible, so Velcro® is the perfect solution.

Related invention

Gideon Sundback invented the modern zipper in 1913.

Conclusion

Inventions are created because someone saw a need. Erik Rotheim needed a way to apply wax to his skis, so he invented the aerosol can. Earle Dickinson saw that his wife needed a bandage strip that would stay in place. Both of these inventions came about because people saw a need and created a product to meet that need.

There is always a need for new inventions to be made. Have a look around you. You might see a need. What kind of product could you make to meet that need? How could you develop it?

You never know, someone might use it to help them around the home in the future.

Index

Activities

Genre Focus

Recount

A recount is a text that tells about something from the past. Recounts can be personal, factual, literary or historical.

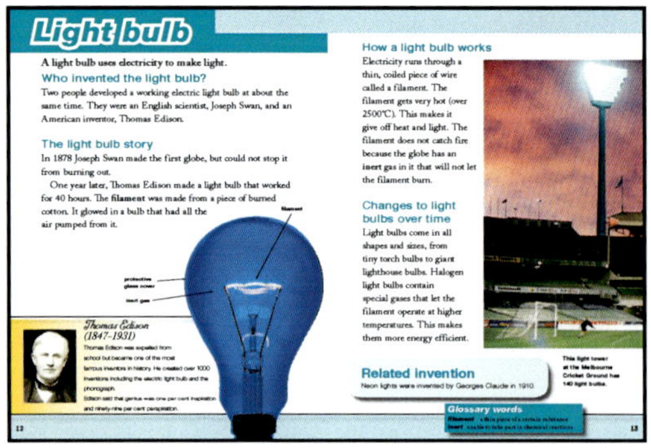

Looking back at a RECOUNT

You will have discovered that *Inventions that Help Us at Home* is made up of a series of factual recounts.

1. A recount begins with an orientation – the reader learns who was involved, what happened, where this event took place and when it happened. Rule up a four-column chart as follows and record the name of each invention in the text, the inventor and when and where it was invented.

Invention	Inventor	Country	Year of Invention

2. The orientation is followed by a chronologically ordered set of events. Choose one of the inventions and using numbered points explain the process of invention. Begin with:

    _____________ invented _____________ by:

3. Most recounts end with a conclusion. Look at the invention of sticky tape on pages 22 and 23. In your own words tell how the author concluded this recount.

4. Language features of a factual recount include: i) past tense ii) words related to time iii) action verbs iv) topic-specific words. Look back at pages 12 and 13. Draw the outline of a lightbulb and divide it into four sections. Fill the sections with examples from the text for each of the above features.

Writing a Recount

1. Think of an invention you would find hard to live without. Use different sources to research its invention. Take notes in point form as you research.

2. Looking back at your notes write an introduction to a factual recount by telling the name of the invention, who invented it and when and where it was invented.

3. Now, on your notes number, in order, the stages the person went through to come up with the invention. Use this information to write a chronologically ordered series of events that led to the invention. You do not need to write the numbers, they are just to get the order correct.

4. Conclude your recount by making a comment about the benefits of the invention.

5. Reread your recount to see if you have used past tense, action verbs, words related to time and special topic words.

Comprehension Focus

Main Idea

Remember

The main idea in a text is the overall message and purpose of the text.

1. To identify some of the main ideas in this text, write and complete the sentences in column A by adding the correct ending from column B.

COLUMN A	COLUMN B
The main idea behind the whole text is that	stops food from sticking.
A BAND-AID®	have been further developed.
Georges de Mestral invented Velcro® when	helps heal wounds and stop infection.
A Teflon® coating on pans	many inventions have made life easier.
Over time, many inventions	he wanted something to attach to fabric the way burrs did to his trousers.

2. Look back at pages 8 and 9. Cut out a circle of card the size of a compact disc. On the card write the main idea presented in these pages. Cut out smaller circles and on each write details that support this main idea. String them together to make a mobile.

3. Fold a piece of card to resemble a refrigerator. On the outside of the door write: 'Frozen food lasts longer'. Rule up shelves inside and on each write a passage of text that supports this main idea.